# Vitamix

## Smoothie

### Recipes

100+ Quick, Healthy, and Delicious Smoothies to Boost Energy,
Support Weight Loss, and Nourish Your Body Every Day

Heather P. Vanburen

This book is for informational purposes only. The author and publisher are not responsible for any adverse effects or consequences resulting from the use of any recipes, suggestions, or procedures described herein. Please consult a qualified health professional before making any significant changes to your diet, especially if you have existing health conditions.

# Table of Contents

# Introduction

Welcome to the *Vitamix Smoothie Recipe Book for Beginners*!

In today's fast-paced world, finding quick, delicious, and health-boosting meal options can feel like a challenge. That's where your Vitamix blender — and this book — come in! Whether you're a busy parent, a fitness enthusiast, a health-conscious foodie, or simply someone eager to add more vibrant, nutrient-rich foods to your life, smoothies are the perfect solution.

With the power of the Vitamix, you can blend ingredients to silky-smooth perfection in seconds — making it easier than ever to nourish your body with wholesome, satisfying smoothies every day.

This book is designed to help you:

- Create smoothies that support your wellness goals, from weight management to energy boosts.
- Save time with simple, fast recipes using everyday ingredients.
- Learn basic blending techniques for achieving the perfect consistency every time.
- Discover creative new flavors while still enjoying classic favorites.

Whether you're brand new to smoothies or looking to take your blending skills to the next level, you'll find a wide variety of recipes in these pages — from green detox blends to protein-packed shakes to decadent dessert smoothies.

**Get ready to experience how a daily smoothie can transform your health, your energy, and your mood. Let's get blending!**

# Article: Why Smoothies are the Ultimate Healthy Habit

Smoothies have become much more than just a trend — they are one of the easiest and most effective ways to support a healthy, vibrant lifestyle. Here's why adding a smoothie a day can be a game changer:

## 1. Packed with Nutrients

A single smoothie can deliver a powerful punch of vitamins, minerals, fiber, and antioxidants. Ingredients like leafy greens, berries, seeds, and nut butters ensure your body gets what it needs to thrive.

## 2. Quick and Convenient

In just a few minutes, you can blend a complete, nourishing meal or snack. No more skipping breakfast or reaching for unhealthy fast food when you're short on time.

## 3. Easy to Digest

Blending breaks down fibers and ingredients, making smoothies easier on your digestive system. This helps your body absorb nutrients faster and more efficiently.

## 4. Customizable for Any Goal

Whether you're looking to lose weight, build muscle, improve gut health, or simply boost your daily fruit and vegetable intake, smoothies can be easily customized to meet your specific needs.

## 5. A Great Way to Sneak in Superfoods

Adding ingredients like chia seeds, flaxseeds, spirulina, or protein powder is an effortless way to boost your nutrient intake without changing the flavor or texture of your smoothie.

## 6. Satisfying and Delicious

Contrary to popular belief, eating healthy doesn't have to be boring. Smoothies can taste like indulgent treats — think chocolate peanut butter, tropical coconut mango, or creamy berry blends — while still being good for you.

In this book, you'll find recipes that make healthy living simple, accessible, and — most importantly — delicious.
With your Vitamix blender by your side, you have the ultimate tool to make every day a little healthier and a lot tastier.

**Cheers to your health and happiness — one smoothie at a time!**

# Tropical Green Smoothie

**Prep Time:** 5 minutes

**Cook Time:** 0 minutes

**Total Time:** 5 minutes

**Servings:** 2

**Ingredients:**

- 1 cup fresh spinach
- 1 cup frozen mango chunks
- 1 banana
- 1/2 cup pineapple chunks (fresh or canned)
- 1 cup coconut water
- 1 tablespoon chia seeds
- 1/2 cup ice (optional)

**Preparation Steps:**

1. Peel and slice the banana, wash and dry the spinach.
2. Fill the Vitamix with spinach and coconut water.
3. Top with banana, pineapple, and mango.
4. Over the fruits, scatter the chia seeds.
5. Turn the blender up from low to high until it's smooth.
6. If desired, add ice and combine once more for a short while.

**Nutritional Information (per serving):**

Calories: 180

Protein: 3g

Carbs: 38g

Fat: 2g

# Berry Protein Smoothie

**Prep Time:** 5 minutes

**Cook Time:** 0 minutes

**Total Time:** 5 minutes

**Servings:** 2

**Ingredients:**

- 1 cup frozen mixed berries
- 1 banana
- 1 scoop vanilla protein powder
- 1 tablespoon almond butter
- 3/4 cup unsweetened almond milk
- 1/2 cup ice

**Preparation Steps:**

1. Slice and peel the banana.
2. Put the banana and almond milk in the Vitamix.
3. Add protein powder and frozen berries.
4. Add almond butter with a spoon.
5. Turn the blender up to high until it's creamy.
6. Blend once more, add ice, and serve.

**Nutritional Information (per serving):**

Calories: 220

Protein: 18g

Carbs: 22g

Fat: 8g

# Peanut Butter Banana Smoothie

**Prep Time:** 5 minutes

**Cook Time:** 0 minutes

**Total Time:** 5 minutes

**Servings:** 2

**Ingredients:**

- 2 ripe bananas
- 2 tablespoons peanut butter
- 1 tablespoon honey
- 1 cup milk (or almond milk)
- 1/2 teaspoon cinnamon
- 1/2 cup ice

**Preparation Steps:**

1. Bananas should be peeled and chopped.
2. Fill the Vitamin with milk.
3. Stir in honey, peanut butter, and bananas.
4. Top with cinnamon.
5. Smoothly blend from low to high.
6. Blend quickly, add ice, and then enjoy.

**Nutritional Information (per serving):**

Calories: 250

Protein: 7g

Carbs: 32g

Fat: 11g

# Pineapple Mint Smoothie

**Prep Time:** 5 minutes

**Cook Time:** 0 minutes

**Total Time:** 5 minutes

**Servings:** 2

**Ingredients:**

- 1 cup pineapple chunks
- 1/2 cup cucumber slices
- 10 fresh mint leaves
- 1/2 cup coconut water
- 1 tablespoon lime juice
- 1/2 cup ice

**Preparation Steps:**

1. Cut the cucumber into tiny bits.
2. Put cucumber and coconut water in the Vitamix.
3. Add the mint leaves and slices of pineapple.
4. Add the lime juice.
5. Smoothly blend from low to high.
6. Blend quickly, add ice, and serve.

**Nutritional Information (per serving):**

Calories: 110

Protein: 1g

Carbs: 25g

Fat: 0g

# Chocolate Avocado Smoothie

**Prep Time:** 5 minutes

**Cook Time:** 0 minutes

**Total Time:** 5 minutes

**Servings:** 2

**Ingredients:**

- 1 ripe avocado
- 1 tablespoon cocoa powder
- 1 tablespoon maple syrup
- 1 cup almond milk
- 1/2 teaspoon vanilla extract
- 1/2 cup ice

**Preparation Steps:**

1. Slice the avocado, scoop out the flesh, and remove the pit.
2. Put the avocado and almond milk in the Vitamix.
3. Add vanilla, maple syrup, and chocolate powder.
4. Turn the blender up to high until it's creamy.
5. Blend with ice until smooth.
6. Transfer to glasses and serve cold.

**Nutritional Information (per serving):**

Calories: 210

Protein: 3g

Carbs: 14g

Fat: 17g

# Mango Lassi Smoothie

**Prep Time:** 5 minutes

**Cook Time:** 0 minutes

**Total Time:** 5 minutes

**Servings:** 2

**Ingredients:**

- 1 cup frozen mango
- 1/2 cup plain yogurt
- 1/2 cup milk
- 1 tablespoon honey
- 1/4 teaspoon ground cardamom
- 1/2 cup ice

**Preparation Steps:**

1. Pour yogurt and milk into the Vitamix.
2. Add honey and frozen mango.
3. On top, scatter the ground cardamom.
4. Until creamy, blend on low and then high.
5. Blend briefly again after adding the ice.
6. Pour into glasses and savor them.

**Nutritional Information (per serving):**

Calories: 180

Protein: 6g

Carbs: 26g

Fat: 4g

# Blueberry Oat Smoothie

**Prep Time:** 5 minutes

**Cook Time:** 0 minutes

**Total Time:** 5 minutes

**Servings:** 2

**Ingredients:**

- 1 cup frozen blueberries
- 1/4 cup rolled oats
- 1 banana
- 1 cup almond milk
- 1 tablespoon flaxseeds
- 1/2 cup ice

**Preparation Steps:**

1. Cut the banana into pieces.
2. Put the banana and almond milk in the Vitamix.
3. Add flaxseeds, oats, and blueberries.
4. Turn the blender from low to high.
5. Blend briefly after adding the ice.
6. For optimal flavor, serve right away.

**Nutritional Information (per serving):**

Calories: 200

Protein: 5g

Carbs: 32g

Fat: 5g

# Strawberry Banana Smoothie

**Prep Time:** 5 minutes

**Cook Time:** 0 minutes

**Total Time:** 5 minutes

**Servings:** 2

**Ingredients:**

- 1 cup frozen strawberries
- 1 banana
- 1/2 cup Greek yogurt
- 3/4 cup almond milk
- 1 tablespoon honey
- 1/2 cup ice

**Preparation Steps:**

1. Slice and peel the banana.
2. Fill the Vitamix with yogurt and almond milk.
3. Add the honey, banana, and strawberries.
4. Smoothly blend from low to high.
5. Blend with ice until foamy.
6. Serve cold through a straw.

**Nutritional Information (per serving):**

Calories: 210

Protein: 8g

Carbs: 30g

Fat: 4g

# Cucumber Apple Detox Smoothie

**Prep Time:** 5 minutes

**Cook Time:** 0 minutes

**Total Time:** 5 minutes

**Servings:** 2

**Ingredients:**

- 1/2 cucumber, chopped
- 1 green apple, cored and sliced
- 1 cup spinach
- 1 tablespoon lemon juice
- 1 cup water
- 1/2 cup ice

**Preparation Steps:**

1. Slice and core the apple.
2. Fill the Vitamix with water and spinach.
3. Add pieces of apple and cucumber.
4. Add the lemon juice.
5. From low to high, blend until smooth.
6. Blend once more, add ice, and savor.

**Nutritional Information (per serving):**

Calories: 90

Protein: 2g

Carbs: 22g

Fat: 0g

# Orange Creamsicle Smoothie

**Prep Time:** 5 minutes

**Cook Time:** 0 minutes

**Total Time:** 5 minutes

**Servings:** 2

**Ingredients:**

- 2 oranges, peeled and segmented
- 1/2 cup vanilla yogurt
- 1/2 cup almond milk
- 1 teaspoon honey (optional)
- 1/2 teaspoon vanilla extract
- 1/2 cup ice

**Preparation Steps:**

1. Oranges should be peeled and segmented.
2. Fill the Vitamix with yogurt and almond milk.
3. Add honey and orange segments.
4. Top with vanilla extract.
5. From low to high, blend until creamy.
6. Blend once more for ten seconds after adding ice.

**Nutritional Information (per serving):**

Calories: 160

Protein: 5g

Carbs: 28g

Fat: 3g

# Kiwi Pineapple Smoothie

**Prep Time:** 5 minutes

**Cook Time:** 0 minutes

**Total Time:** 5 minutes

**Servings:** 2

**Ingredients:**

- 2 ripe kiwis, peeled
- 1 cup pineapple chunks
- 1/2 cup coconut water
- 1/2 cup Greek yogurt
- 1 tablespoon honey
- 1/2 cup ice

**Preparation Steps:**

1. Cut the kiwis into pieces after peeling them.
2. Fill the Vitamix with Greek yogurt and coconut water.
3. Add the pineapple, honey, and kiwi.
4. Start on low and work your way up to high.
5. Blend with ice until smooth.
6. Garnish with mint and serve cold.

**Nutritional Information (per serving):**

Calories: 160

Protein: 6g

Carbs: 35g

Fat: 2g

# Apple Cinnamon Smoothie

**Prep Time:** 5 minutes

**Cook Time:** 0 minutes

**Total Time:** 5 minutes

**Servings:** 2

**Ingredients:**

- 2 apples, cored and sliced
- 1/2 teaspoon ground cinnamon
- 1 tablespoon honey
- 1 cup almond milk
- 1/4 cup oats
- 1/2 cup ice

**Preparation Steps:**

1. Cut apples into pieces after coreing them.
2. Fill the Vitamix with oats and almond milk.
3. Stir in honey, cinnamon, and apples.
4. Turn the blender up to high after blending on low.
5. Blend with ice until foamy.
6. Garnish with cinnamon and serve cold.

**Nutritional Information (per serving):**

Calories: 190

Protcin: 4g

Carbs: 42g

Fat: 4g

# Chocolate Banana Smoothie

**Prep Time:** 5 minutes

**Cook Time:** 0 minutes

**Total Time:** 5 minutes

**Servings:** 2

**Ingredients:**

- 2 bananas
- 1 tablespoon cocoa powder
- 1 tablespoon peanut butter
- 1 cup milk
- 1 teaspoon vanilla extract
- 1/2 cup ice

**Preparation Steps:**

1. Slice and peel bananas.
2. Put peanut butter and milk in the Vitamix.
3. Add vanilla, bananas, and chocolate powder.
4. Start low and work your way up to high.
5. Blend with ice until smooth.
6. Pour into glasses and savor them.

**Nutritional Information (per serving):**

Calories: 230

Protein: 6g

Carbs: 32g

Fat: 9g

# Mango Coconut Smoothie

**Prep Time:** 5 minutes

**Cook Time:** 0 minutes

**Total Time:** 5 minutes

**Servings:** 2

**Ingredients:**

- 1 cup frozen mango
- 1/2 cup coconut milk
- 1/2 cup pineapple juice
- 1/4 cup shredded coconut
- 1 tablespoon honey
- 1/2 cup ice

**Preparation Steps:**

1. Pour pineapple juice and coconut milk into the Vitamix.
2. Add the shredded coconut and frozen mango.
3. Add honey with a spoon for sweetness.
4. Start low and work your way up to high.
5. Blend till creamy after adding ice.
6. Top with additional shredded coconut and serve.

**Nutritional Information (per serving):**

Calories: 210

Protein: 2g

Carbs: 50g

Fat: 8g

# Green Apple Kale Smoothie

**Prep Time:** 5 minutes

**Cook Time:** 0 minutes

**Total Time:** 5 minutes

**Servings:** 2

**Ingredients:**

- 1 green apple, cored and sliced
- 1 cup kale leaves
- 1/2 cup almond milk
- 1 tablespoon chia seeds
- 1/2 teaspoon lemon juice
- 1/2 cup ice

**Preparation Steps:**

1. Slice and core the green apple.
2. Put the greens and almond milk in the Vitamix.
3. Stir in lemon juice, chia seeds, and apple slices.
4. Turn the blender up to high after blending on low.
5. Blend with ice until smooth.
6. Garnish with more chia seeds and serve cold.

**Nutritional Information (per serving):**

Calories: 150

Protein: 4g

Carbs: 34g

Fat: 4g

# Papaya Ginger Smoothie

**Prep Time:** 5 minutes

**Cook Time:** 0 minutes

**Total Time:** 5 minutes

**Servings:** 2

**Ingredients:**

- 1 cup papaya chunks
- 1 tablespoon fresh ginger, grated
- 1/2 cup coconut water
- 1 tablespoon honey
- 1/2 cup Greek yogurt
- 1/2 cup ice

**Preparation Steps:**

1. Fill the Vitamix with Greek yogurt and coconut water.
2. Add grated ginger and papaya chunks.
3. Add honey with a spoon for sweetness.
4. Start on low and work your way up to high.
5. Blend with ice until smooth.
6. Garnish with mint and serve cold.

**Nutritional Information (per serving):**

Calories: 180

Protein: 6g

Carbs: 39g

Fat: 3g

# Avocado Pineapple Smoothie

**Prep Time:** 5 minutes

**Cook Time:** 0 minutes

**Total Time:** 5 minutes

**Servings:** 2

**Ingredients:**

- 1 ripe avocado
- 1 cup pineapple chunks
- 1/2 cup coconut milk
- 1 tablespoon lime juice
- 1 teaspoon honey
- 1/2 cup ice

**Preparation Steps:**

1. Slice the avocado, scoop out the flesh, and remove the pit.
2. Put the avocado and coconut milk in the Vitamix.
3. Add the lime juice and slices of pineapple.
4. Start on low and work your way up to high.
5. Blend in ice and honey until smooth.
6. Serve cold, garnished with a wedge of lime.

**Nutritional Information (per serving):**

Calories: 220

Protein: 3g

Carbs: 29g

Fat: 15g

# Raspberry Peach Smoothie

**Prep Time:** 5 minutes

**Cook Time:** 0 minutes

**Total Time:** 5 minutes

**Servings:** 2

**Ingredients:**

- 1 cup frozen raspberries
- 1 cup frozen peach slices
- 1/2 cup Greek yogurt
- 1 tablespoon honey
- 3/4 cup almond milk
- 1/2 cup ice

**Preparation Steps:**

1. Fill the Vitamix with Greek yogurt and almond milk.
2. Add slices of peach and frozen raspberries.
3. Add honey with a spoon for sweetness.
4. Smoothly blend on low to high.
5. Blend once more after adding ice.
6. Garnish with fresh berries and serve cold.

**Nutritional Information (per serving):**

Calories: 180

Protein: 6g

Carbs: 33g

Fat: 4g

# Cantaloupe Mint Smoothie

**Prep Time:** 5 minutes

**Cook Time:** 0 minutes

**Total Time:** 5 minutes

**Servings:** 2

**Ingredients:**

- 1 cup cantaloupe chunks
- 10 fresh mint leaves
- 1/2 cup coconut water
- 1 tablespoon honey
- 1/2 teaspoon lime juice
- 1/2 cup ice

**Preparation Steps:**

1. Pour lime juice and coconut water into the Vitamix.
2. Add the mint leaves and slices of cantaloupe.
3. Add honey with a spoon for sweetness.
4. Smoothly blend on low to high.
5. Blend briefly after adding the ice.
6. Garnish with mint and serve cold.

**Nutritional Information (per serving):**

Calories: 140

Protein: 2g

Carbs: 35g

Fat: 0g

# Dragon Fruit Smoothie

**Prep Time:** 5 minutes

**Cook Time:** 0 minutes

**Total Time:** 5 minutes

**Servings:** 2

**Ingredients:**

- 1 cup frozen dragon fruit
- 1/2 banana
- 1/2 cup coconut water
- 1 tablespoon honey
- 1/2 cup almond milk
- 1/2 cup ice

**Preparation Steps:**

1. Fill the Vitamix with almond milk and coconut water.
2. Add banana slices with frozen dragon fruit.
3. Add honey with a spoon for sweetness.
4. Smoothly blend on low to high.
5. Blend with ice until foamy.
6. Garnish with coconut flakes and serve cold.

**Nutritional Information (per serving):**

Calories: 160

Protein: 3g

Carbs: 35g

Fat: 3g

# Blueberry Almond Smoothie

**Prep Time:** 5 minutes

**Cook Time:** 0 minutes

**Total Time:** 5 minutes

**Servings:** 2

**Ingredients:**

- 1 cup frozen blueberries
- 1 tablespoon almond butter
- 1 cup almond milk
- 1/2 teaspoon cinnamon
- 1 tablespoon honey
- 1/2 cup ice

**Preparation Steps:**

1. Fill the Vitamix with almond butter and milk.
2. Add cinnamon and frozen blueberries.
3. Add honey with a spoon for sweetness.
4. Start with a low blend and work your way up to high.
5. Blend with ice until smooth.
6. Garnish with cinnamon and serve cold.

**Nutritional Information (per serving):**

Calories: 210

Protein: 5g

Carbs: 30g

Fat: 10g

# Strawberry Mango Smoothie

**Prep Time:** 5 minutes

**Cook Time:** 0 minutes

**Total Time:** 5 minutes

**Servings:** 2

**Ingredients:**

- 1 cup frozen strawberries
- 1 cup frozen mango
- 1/2 cup orange juice
- 1/2 cup Greek yogurt
- 1 tablespoon honey
- 1/2 cup ice

**Preparation Steps:**

1. Fill the Vitamix with Greek yogurt and orange juice.
2. Add the mango and frozen strawberries.
3. Add honey with a spoon for sweetness.
4. Smoothly blend on low to high.
5. Blend once more after adding ice.
6. Garnish with mint and serve cold.

**Nutritional Information (per serving):**

Calories: 190

Protein: 6g

Carbs: 40g

Fat: 4g

# Pear Ginger Smoothie

**Prep Time:** 5 minutes

**Cook Time:** 0 minutes

**Total Time:** 5 minutes

**Servings:** 2

**Ingredients:**

- 2 ripe pears, cored and sliced
- 1/2 teaspoon fresh ginger, grated
- 1 tablespoon honey
- 1/2 cup almond milk
- 1/4 teaspoon vanilla extract
- 1/2 cup ice

**Preparation Steps:**

1. Slice and core the pears.
2. Fill the Vitamix with almond milk and vanilla essence.
3. Add the grated ginger and pears.
4. Add honey with a spoon for sweetness.
5. Smoothly blend on low to high.
6. Blend till creamy after adding ice.

**Nutritional Information (per serving):**

Calories: 160

Protein: 2g

Carbs: 41g

Fat: 4g

# Watermelon Lime Smoothie

**Prep Time:** 5 minutes

**Cook Time:** 0 minutes

**Total Time:** 5 minutes

**Servings:** 2

**Ingredients:**

- 2 cups watermelon chunks
- 1 tablespoon lime juice
- 1/2 cup coconut water
- 1 tablespoon honey
- 1/2 cup ice

**Preparation Steps:**

1. Pour lime juice and coconut water into the Vitamix.
2. Add honey and slices of watermelon.
3. Start with a low blend and work your way up to high.
4. Blend with ice until smooth.
5. If necessary, taste and add additional honey.
6. Serve cold, garnished with a wedge of lime.

**Nutritional Information (per serving):**

Calories: 140

Protein: 2g

Carbs: 35g

Fat: 0g

# Orange Creamsicle Smoothie

**Prep Time:** 5 minutes

**Cook Time:** 0 minutes

**Total Time:** 5 minutes

**Servings:** 2

**Ingredients:**

- 1 cup orange juice
- 1/2 cup Greek yogurt
- 1/4 teaspoon vanilla extract
- 1 tablespoon honey
- 1/2 cup ice

**Preparation Steps:**

1. Fill the Vitamix with Greek yogurt and orange juice.
2. Add honey and vanilla extract.
3. Start on low and work your way up to high.
4. Blend with ice until smooth.
5. If desired, add more honey after tasting.
6. Garnish with orange slices and serve cold.

**Nutritional Information (per serving):**

Calories: 180

Protein: 6g

Carbs: 35g

Fat: 4g

# Cherry Almond Smoothie

**Prep Time:** 5 minutes

**Cook Time:** 0 minutes

**Total Time:** 5 minutes

**Servings:** 2

**Ingredients:**

- 1 cup frozen cherries
- 1 tablespoon almond butter
- 1/2 cup almond milk
- 1 tablespoon honey
- 1/4 teaspoon cinnamon
- 1/2 cup ice

**Preparation Steps:**

1. Fill the Vitamix with almond butter and milk.
2. Add cinnamon and frozen cherries.
3. Add honey with a spoon for sweetness.
4. Smoothly blend on low to high.
5. Blend till creamy after adding ice.
6. Garnish with cinnamon and serve cold.

**Nutritional Information (per serving):**

Calories: 210

Protein: 5g

Carbs: 30g

Fat: 11g

# Pomegranate Blueberry Smoothie

**Prep Time:** 5 minutes

**Cook Time:** 0 minutes

**Total Time:** 5 minutes

**Servings:** 2

**Ingredients:**

- 1 cup pomegranate seeds
- 1/2 cup frozen blueberries
- 1 cup almond milk
- 1 tablespoon honey
- 1/2 cup ice

**Preparation Steps:**

1. Put the pomegranate seeds and almond milk in the Vitamix.
2. Add honey and frozen blueberries.
3. Start on low and work your way up to high.
4. Blend with ice until smooth.
5. If necessary, taste and add additional honey to adjust sweetness.
6. Garnish with additional pomegranate seeds and serve cold.

**Nutritional Information (per serving):**

Calories: 180

Protein: 4g

Carbs: 40g

Fat: 4g

# Spiced Apple Smoothie

**Prep Time:** 5 minutes

**Cook Time:** 0 minutes

**Total Time:** 5 minutes

**Servings:** 2

**Ingredients:**

- 2 apples, cored and sliced
- 1/2 teaspoon ground cinnamon
- 1/4 teaspoon ground nutmeg
- 1/2 cup almond milk
- 1 tablespoon honey
- 1/2 cup ice

**Preparation Steps:**

1. Slice and core apples.
2. In Vitamix, add nutmeg, cinnamon, and almond milk.
3. Add honey and apple slices.
4. Smoothly blend on low to high.
5. Blend with ice until foamy.
6. Garnish with cinnamon and serve cold.

**Nutritional Information (per serving):**

Calories: 170

Protein: 2g

Carbs: 43g

Fat: 4g

# Pineapple Peach Smoothie

**Prep Time:** 5 minutes

**Cook Time:** 0 minutes

**Total Time:** 5 minutes

**Servings:** 2

**Ingredients:**

- 1 cup frozen pineapple chunks
- 1 cup frozen peach slices
- 1/2 cup coconut water
- 1/2 cup Greek yogurt
- 1 tablespoon honey
- 1/2 cup ice

**Preparation Steps:**

1. Fill the Vitamix with Greek yogurt and coconut water.
2. Add pieces of peach and frozen pineapple.
3. Add honey with a spoon for sweetness.
4. Smoothly blend on low to high.
5. Blend once more after adding ice.
6. Serve cold, accompanied by a peach slice.

**Nutritional Information (per serving):**

Calories: 180

Protein: 6g

Carbs: 39g

Fat: 4g

# Cucumber Mint Smoothie

**Prep Time:** 5 minutes

**Cook Time:** 0 minutes

**Total Time:** 5 minutes

**Servings:** 2

**Ingredients:**

- 1 cucumber, peeled and sliced
- 10 fresh mint leaves
- 1/2 cup Greek yogurt
- 1 tablespoon honey
- 1/2 cup water
- 1/2 cup ice

**Preparation Steps:**

1. Slice and peel the cucumber.
2. Fill the Vitamix with water and Greek yogurt.
3. Add fresh mint leaves and cucumber.
4. Add honey with a spoon for sweetness.
5. Smoothly blend on low to high.
6. Blend with ice until foamy.

**Nutritional Information (per serving):**

Calories: 150

Protein: 6g

Carbs: 22g

Fat: 4g

# Tropical Green Smoothie

**Prep Time:** 5 minutes

**Cook Time:** 0 minutes

**Total Time:** 5 minutes

**Servings:** 2

**Ingredients:**

- 1 cup frozen pineapple chunks
- 1/2 banana
- 1/2 cup spinach
- 1/2 cup coconut water
- 1 tablespoon chia seeds
- 1/2 cup ice

**Preparation Steps:**

1. Put spinach and coconut water in the Vitamix.
2. Add the banana, chia seeds, and frozen pineapple.
3. Smoothly blend on low to high.
4. Blend till creamy after adding ice.
5. If necessary, taste and add additional banana to balance the sweetness.
6. Garnish with additional chia seeds and serve cold.

**Nutritional Information (per serving):**

Calories: 160

Protein: 3g

Carbs: 36g

Fat: 5g

# Acai Berry Smoothie

**Prep Time:** 5 minutes

**Cook Time:** 0 minutes

**Total Time:** 5 minutes

**Servings:** 2

**Ingredients:**

- 1 packet frozen acai berry puree
- 1/2 cup frozen strawberries
- 1/2 banana
- 1/2 cup almond milk
- 1 tablespoon honey
- 1/2 cup ice

**Preparation Steps:**

1. Fill the Vitamix with the acai berry puree and almond milk.
2. Add the banana and frozen strawberries.
3. Add honey with a spoon for sweetness.
4. Smoothly blend on low to high.
5. Blend till creamy after adding ice.
6. Garnish with granola and serve chilled.

**Nutritional Information (per serving):**

Calories: 190

Protein: 4g

Carbs: 38g

Fat: 5g

# Chocolate Banana Smoothie

**Prep Time:** 5 minutes

**Cook Time:** 0 minutes

**Total Time:** 5 minutes

**Servings:** 2

**Ingredients:**

- 1 banana
- 1 tablespoon cocoa powder
- 1 tablespoon peanut butter
- 1 cup almond milk
- 1 tablespoon honey
- 1/2 cup ice

**Preparation Steps:**

1. Put peanut butter and almond milk in the Vitamix.
2. Add the chocolate powder and banana.
3. Add honey with a spoon for sweetness.
4. Smoothly blend on low to high.
5. Blend till creamy after adding ice.
6. Top with a peanut butter drizzle and serve cold.

**Nutritional Information (per serving):**

Calories: 210

Protein: 6g

Carbs: 33g

Fat: 8g

# Kiwi Strawberry Smoothie

**Prep Time:** 5 minutes

**Cook Time:** 0 minutes

**Total Time:** 5 minutes

**Servings:** 2

**Ingredients:**

- 2 ripe kiwis, peeled and sliced
- 1 cup frozen strawberries
- 1/2 cup orange juice
- 1/2 cup Greek yogurt
- 1 tablespoon honey
- 1/2 cup ice

**Preparation Steps:**

1. Slice and peel the kiwis.
2. Fill the Vitamix with Greek yogurt and orange juice.
3. Add the cut kiwis and frozen strawberries.
4. Add honey with a spoon for sweetness.
5. Smoothly blend on low to high.
6. Blend once more until creamy after adding ice.

**Nutritional Information (per serving):**

Calories: 180

Protein: 6g

Carbs: 38g

Fat: 4g

# Pear Pineapple Smoothie

**Prep Time:** 5 minutes

**Cook Time:** 0 minutes

**Total Time:** 5 minutes

**Servings:** 2

**Ingredients:**

- 1 pear, cored and sliced
- 1 cup frozen pineapple chunks
- 1/2 cup coconut water
- 1/2 cup Greek yogurt
- 1 tablespoon honey
- 1/2 cup ice

**Preparation Steps:**

1. Slice and core the pear.
2. Fill the Vitamix with Greek yogurt and coconut water.
3. Add slices of pear and chunks of frozen pineapple.
4. Add honey with a spoon for sweetness.
5. Smoothly blend on low to high.
6. Blend till creamy after adding ice.

**Nutritional Information (per serving):**

Calories: 170

Protein: 6g

Carbs: 38g

Fat: 4g

# Raspberry Lemonade Smoothie

**Prep Time:** 5 minutes

**Cook Time:** 0 minutes

**Total Time:** 5 minutes

**Servings:** 2

**Ingredients:**

- 1 cup frozen raspberries
- 1 tablespoon lemon juice
- 1/2 cup almond milk
- 1 tablespoon honey
- 1/2 cup ice

**Preparation Steps:**

1. Pour lemon juice and almond milk into the Vitamix.
2. Add honey and frozen raspberries.
3. Smoothly blend on low to high.
4. Blend with ice until foamy.
5. If necessary, taste and add additional honey.
6. Garnish with a lemon wedge and serve cold.

**Nutritional Information (per serving):**

Calories: 160

Protein: 3g

Carbs: 36g

Fat: 4g

# Carrot Ginger Smoothie

**Prep Time:** 5 minutes

**Cook Time:** 0 minutes

**Total Time:** 5 minutes

**Servings:** 2

**Ingredients:**

- 2 medium carrots, peeled and chopped
- 1/2 teaspoon fresh ginger, grated
- 1/2 cup orange juice
- 1/2 cup almond milk
- 1 tablespoon honey
- 1/2 cup ice

**Preparation Steps:**

1. Chop and peel the carrots.
2. Fill the Vitamix with almond milk and orange juice.
3. Add grated ginger and diced carrots.
4. Add honey with a spoon for sweetness.
5. Smoothly blend on low to high.
6. Blend with ice until foamy.

**Nutritional Information (per serving):**

Calories: 170

Protein: 3g

Carbs: 40g

Fat: 4g

# Pumpkin Spice Smoothie

**Prep Time:** 5 minutes

**Cook Time:** 0 minutes

**Total Time:** 5 minutes

**Servings:** 2

**Ingredients:**

- 1/2 cup canned pumpkin puree
- 1/2 banana
- 1/2 cup almond milk
- 1/2 teaspoon cinnamon
- 1/4 teaspoon nutmeg
- 1 tablespoon maple syrup
- 1/2 cup ice

**Preparation Steps:**

1. Fill the Vitamix with canned pumpkin and almond milk.
2. Add nutmeg, cinnamon, and banana.
3. Add maple syrup with a spoon for sweetness.
4. Smoothly blend on low to high.
5. Blend till creamy after adding ice.
6. Garnish with cinnamon and serve cold.

**Nutritional Information (per serving):**

Calories: 180

Protein: 3g

Carbs: 41g

Fat: 4g

# Avocado Mint Smoothie

**Prep Time:** 5 minutes

**Cook Time:** 0 minutes

**Total Time:** 5 minutes

**Servings:** 2

**Ingredients:**

- 1 ripe avocado, peeled and pitted
- 10 fresh mint leaves
- 1/2 cup coconut water
- 1 tablespoon honey
- 1/2 cup ice

**Preparation Steps:**

1. Pit and peel the avocado.
2. Fill the Vitamix with coconut water.
3. Add fresh mint leaves and avocado.
4. Add honey with a spoon for sweetness.
5. Smoothly blend on low to high.
6. Blend till creamy after adding ice.

**Nutritional Information (per serving):**

Calories: 230

Protein: 3g

Carbs: 20g

Fat: 18g

# Sweet Potato Pie Smoothie

**Prep Time:** 5 minutes

**Cook Time:** 0 minutes

**Total Time:** 5 minutes

**Servings:** 2

**Ingredients:**

- 1/2 cup cooked sweet potato
- 1/2 cup almond milk
- 1/2 teaspoon cinnamon
- 1/4 teaspoon nutmeg
- 1 tablespoon maple syrup
- 1/2 cup ice

**Preparation Steps:**

1. Put the cooked sweet potato and almond milk in the Vitamix.
2. Add maple syrup, nutmeg, and cinnamon.
3. Smoothly blend on low to high.
4. Blend till creamy after adding ice.
5. If necessary, taste and add additional maple syrup.
6. Garnish with cinnamon and serve cold.

**Nutritional Information (per serving):**

Calories: 190

Protein: 4g

Carbs: 42g

Fat: 4g

# Pomegranate Blueberry Smoothie

**Prep Time:** 5 minutes

**Cook Time:** 0 minutes

**Total Time:** 5 minutes

**Servings:** 2

**Ingredients:**

- 1/2 cup frozen blueberries
- 1/2 cup pomegranate seeds
- 1/2 banana
- 1/2 cup almond milk
- 1 tablespoon honey
- 1/2 cup ice

**Preparation Steps:**

1. Put the pomegranate seeds and almond milk in the Vitamix.
2. Add the banana and frozen blueberries.
3. Add honey with a spoon for sweetness.
4. Smoothly blend on low to high.
5. Blend with ice until foamy.
6. Top with additional pomegranate seeds and serve cold.

**Nutritional Information (per serving):**

Calories: 180

Protein: 3g

Carbs: 38g

Fat: 4g

# Mango Coconut Smoothie

**Prep Time:** 5 minutes

**Cook Time:** 0 minutes

**Total Time:** 5 minutes

**Servings:** 2

**Ingredients:**

- 1 cup frozen mango chunks
- 1/2 banana
- 1/2 cup coconut milk
- 1 tablespoon shredded coconut
- 1 tablespoon honey
- 1/2 cup ice

**Preparation Steps:**

1. Put the shredded coconut and coconut milk in the Vitamix.
2. Add the banana and frozen mango chunks.
3. Add honey with a spoon for sweetness.
4. Smoothly blend on low to high.
5. Blend till creamy after adding ice.
6. Garnish with shredded coconut and serve chilled.

**Nutritional Information (per serving):**

Calories: 210

Protein: 3g

Carbs: 42g

Fat: 6g

# Watermelon Mint Smoothie

**Prep Time:** 5 minutes

**Cook Time:** 0 minutes

**Total Time:** 5 minutes

**Servings:** 2

**Ingredients:**

- 2 cups watermelon chunks
- 10 fresh mint leaves
- 1/2 cup coconut water
- 1 tablespoon honey
- 1/2 cup ice

**Preparation Steps:**

1. Put the mint leaves and coconut water in the Vitamix.
2. Add honey and slices of watermelon.
3. Smoothly blend on low to high.
4. Blend with ice until foamy.
5. If desired, taste and add additional honey to adjust sweetness.
6. Serve cold, garnished with a sprig of mint.

**Nutritional Information (per serving):**

Calories: 140

Protein: 2g

Carbs: 35g

Fat: 0g

# Pineapple Ginger Smoothie

**Prep Time:** 5 minutes

**Cook Time:** 0 minutes

**Total Time:** 5 minutes

**Servings:** 2

**Ingredients:**

- 1 cup frozen pineapple chunks
- 1/2 teaspoon fresh ginger, grated
- 1/2 banana
- 1/2 cup coconut water
- 1 tablespoon honey
- 1/2 cup ice

**Preparation Steps:**

1. To Vitamix, blend coconut water and fresh ginger.
2. Add the frozen bananas and pineapple.
3. Sweetness in honey comes from spoon-in.
4. Blend low to high till smooth.
5. Add ice and whirl until creamy.
6. Present cold together with a slice of pineapple.

**Nutritional Information (per serving):**

Calories: 180

Protein: 3g

Carbs: 38g

Fat: 4g

# Chocolate Peanut Butter Smoothie

**Prep Time:** 5 minutes

**Cook Time:** 0 minutes

**Total Time:** 5 minutes

**Servings:** 2

**Ingredients:**

- 1 banana
- 1 tablespoon cocoa powder
- 1 tablespoon peanut butter
- 1 cup almond milk
- 1 tablespoon honey
- 1/2 cup ice

**Preparation Steps:**

1. Put peanut butter and almond milk in the Vitamix.
2. Blend in the chocolate powder and banana.
3. To make it sweeter, spoon in some honey.
4. Blend on low until completely smooth.
5. Blend in the ice until smooth and creamy.
6. Top with a little peanut butter and serve cold.

**Nutritional Information (per serving):**

Calories: 210

Protein: 6g

Carbs: 30g

Fat: 9g

# Papaya Lime Smoothie

**Prep Time:** 5 minutes

**Cook Time:** 0 minutes

**Total Time:** 5 minutes

**Servings:** 2

**Ingredients:**

- 1 cup papaya chunks
- 1/2 banana
- 1 tablespoon lime juice
- 1/2 cup coconut water
- 1 tablespoon honey
- 1/2 cup ice

**Preparation Steps:**

1. Incorporate lime juice and coconut water into the Vitamix.
2. Combine with banana and papaya chunks.
3. To make it sweeter, spoon in some honey.
4. Blend on low until completely smooth.
5. Blend in the ice until smooth and creamy.
6. Garnish with a wedge of lime and serve cold.

**Nutritional Information (per serving):**

Calories: 160

Protein: 2g

Carbs: 38g

Fat: 4g

# Cherry Almond Smoothie

**Prep Time:** 5 minutes

**Cook Time:** 0 minutes

**Total Time:** 5 minutes

**Servings:** 2

**Ingredients:**

- 1 cup frozen cherries
- 1/2 banana
- 1 tablespoon almond butter
- 1 cup almond milk
- 1 tablespoon honey
- 1/2 cup ice

**Preparation Steps:**

1. To the Vitamix, add almond butter and almond milk.
2. Incorporate the banana and frozen cherries.
3. To make it sweeter, spoon in some honey.
4. Blend on low until completely smooth.
5. Blend in the ice until smooth and creamy.
6. Drizzle sliced almonds over top before serving cold.

**Nutritional Information (per serving):**

Calories: 190

Protein: 4g

Carbs: 38g

Fat: 7g

# Strawberry Kiwi Smoothie

**Prep Time:** 5 minutes

**Cook Time:** 0 minutes

**Total Time:** 5 minutes

**Servings:** 2

**Ingredients:**

- 1 cup frozen strawberries
- 2 kiwis, peeled and sliced
- 1/2 cup orange juice
- 1/2 cup Greek yogurt
- 1 tablespoon honey
- 1/2 cup ice

**Preparation Steps:**

1. Incorporate Greek yogurt and orange juice into the Vitamix.
2. Toss in some sliced kiwis and frozen strawberries.
3. To make it sweeter, spoon in some honey.
4. Blend on low until completely smooth.
5. Blend in the ice until smooth and creamy.
6. Present cold, garnished with a kiwi slice.

**Nutritional Information (per serving):**

Calories: 170

Protein: 6g

Carbs: 38g

Fat: 4g

# Peach Coconut Smoothie

**Prep Time:** 5 minutes

**Cook Time:** 0 minutes

**Total Time:** 5 minutes

**Servings:** 2

**Ingredients:**

- 1 cup frozen peaches
- 1/2 banana
- 1/2 cup coconut milk
- 1 tablespoon shredded coconut
- 1 tablespoon honey
- 1/2 cup ice

**Preparation Steps:**

1. Put the shredded coconut and coconut milk into the Vitamix.
2. Combine the banana and frozen peaches.
3. To make it sweeter, spoon in some honey.
4. Blend on low until completely smooth.
5. Blend in the ice until smooth and creamy.
6. Serve cold and garnish with additional coconut flakes.

**Nutritional Information (per serving):**

Calories: 190

Protein: 3g

Carbs: 36g

Fat: 7g

# Cucumber Melon Smoothie

**Prep Time:** 5 minutes

**Cook Time:** 0 minutes

**Total Time:** 5 minutes

**Servings:** 2

**Ingredients:**

- 1 cup honeydew melon chunks
- 1/2 cucumber, peeled and chopped
- 1 tablespoon lime juice
- 1/2 cup coconut water
- 1 tablespoon honey
- 1/2 cup ice

**Preparation Steps:**

1. Incorporate lime juice and coconut water into the Vitamix.
2. Toss in some diced cucumber and honeydew melon chunks.
3. To make it sweeter, spoon in some honey.
4. Blend on low until completely smooth.
5. Blend in the ice until it becomes foamy.
6. Accompany with a cucumber slice as a garnish and serve cold.

**Nutritional Information (per serving):**

Calories: 140

Protein: 2g

Carbs: 35g

Fat: 0g

# Blackberry Vanilla Smoothie

**Prep Time:** 5 minutes

**Cook Time:** 0 minutes

**Total Time:** 5 minutes

**Servings:** 2

**Ingredients:**

- 1 cup frozen blackberries
- 1/2 banana
- 1/2 teaspoon vanilla extract
- 1 cup almond milk
- 1 tablespoon honey
- 1/2 cup ice

**Preparation Steps:**

1. Smoothly blend almond milk and vanilla extract in the Vitamix.
2. Incorporate bananas and frozen blackberries.
3. To make it sweeter, spoon in some honey.
4. Blend on low until completely smooth.
5. Blend in the ice until smooth and creamy.
6. Finish with a garnish of fresh blackberries.

**Nutritional Information (per serving):**

Calories: 170

Protein: 3g

Carbs: 35g

Fat: 4g

# Green Goddess Smoothie

**Prep Time:** 5 minutes

**Cook Time:** 0 minutes

**Total Time:** 5 minutes

**Servings:** 2

**Ingredients:**

- 1 cup spinach leaves
- 1/2 avocado
- 1 green apple, sliced
- 1/2 cup cucumber slices
- 1/2 cup coconut water
- 1 tablespoon lemon juice
- 1/2 cup ice

**Preparation Steps:**

1. Blend in the Vitamix with the coconut water and lemon juice.
2. Toss in some cucumber, apple, spinach, and avocado.
3. Blend on low until completely smooth.
4. Blend in the ice until smooth and creamy.
5. Adjust the lemon according to your taste.
6. Add a slice of cucumber for garnish.

**Nutritional Information (per serving):**

Calories: 160

Protein: 3g

Carbs: 20g

Fat: 8g

# Raspberry Lemonade Smoothie

**Prep Time:** 5 minutes

**Cook Time:** 0 minutes

**Total Time:** 5 minutes

**Servings:** 2

**Ingredients:**

- 1 cup frozen raspberries
- 1/2 banana
- 1/4 cup lemon juice
- 1 cup cold water
- 1 tablespoon honey
- 1/2 cup ice

**Preparation Steps:**

1. Put the lemon juice and cold water into the Vitamix.
2. Combine the banana with the frozen raspberries.
3. To make it sweeter, spoon in some honey.
4. Blend on low until completely smooth.
5. Blend in the ice until it becomes foamy.
6. Add a slice of lemon for garnish.

**Nutritional Information (per serving):**

Calories: 150

Protein: 2g

Carbs: 32g

Fat: 1g

# Tropical Spinach Smoothie

**Prep Time:** 5 minutes

**Cook Time:** 0 minutes

**Total Time:** 5 minutes

**Servings:** 2

**Ingredients:**

- 1 cup spinach leaves
- 1/2 cup frozen mango chunks
- 1/2 cup frozen pineapple chunks
- 1/2 banana
- 1/2 cup coconut water
- 1/2 cup ice

**Preparation Steps:**

1. Turn on the Vitamix and pour in the coconut water.
2. Toss in some bananas, mangoes, spinach, and pineapple.
3. Blend on low until completely smooth.
4. Blend in the ice until smooth and creamy.
5. If necessary, adjust the sweetness by tasting.
6. Garnish with a sprig of mint and serve cold.

**Nutritional Information (per serving):**

Calories: 170

Protein: 3g

Carbs: 38g

Fat: 2g

# Coffee Banana Smoothie

**Prep Time:** 5 minutes

**Cook Time:** 0 minutes

**Total Time:** 5 minutes

**Servings:** 2

**Ingredients:**

- 1/2 cup brewed coffee, cooled
- 1 banana
- 1/2 cup almond milk
- 1 tablespoon peanut butter
- 1 tablespoon honey
- 1/2 cup ice

**Preparation Steps:**

1. Blend in the Vitamix with the almond milk and coffee.
2. Put in some peanut butter and bananas.
3. To make it sweeter, spoon in some honey.
4. Blend on low until completely smooth.
5. Blend in the ice until smooth and creamy.
6. Sprinkle some chocolate powder on top before serving.

**Nutritional Information (per serving):**

Calories: 190

Protein: 5g

Carbs: 28g

Fat: 7g

# Banana Orange Smoothie

**Prep Time:** 5 minutes

**Cook Time:** 0 minutes

**Total Time:** 5 minutes

**Servings:** 2

**Ingredients:**

- 1 banana
- 1/2 cup orange juice
- 1/2 cup Greek yogurt
- 1 tablespoon honey
- 1/2 cup ice

**Preparation Steps:**

1. Incorporate Greek yogurt and orange juice into the Vitamix.
2. Toss in the honey and banana.
3. Blend on low until completely smooth.
4. Blend in the ice until smooth and creamy.
5. It goes well with a wedge of orange.
6. Optional: top with mint for garnish.

**Nutritional Information (per serving):**

Calories: 180

Protein: 6g

Carbs: 32g

Fat: 4g

# Avocado Blueberry Smoothie

**Prep Time:** 5 minutes

**Cook Time:** 0 minutes

**Total Time:** 5 minutes

**Servings:** 2

**Ingredients:**

- 1/2 avocado
- 1/2 cup frozen blueberries
- 1/2 banana
- 1/2 cup almond milk
- 1 tablespoon honey
- 1/2 cup ice

**Preparation Steps:**

1. Fill the Vitamix with almond milk.
2. Put in some bananas, blueberries, and avocados.
3. To make it sweeter, spoon in some honey.
4. Blend on low until completely smooth.
5. Blend in the ice until smooth and creamy.
6. Toss in some blueberries before serving.

**Nutritional Information (per serving):**

Calories: 190

Protein: 4g

Carbs: 26g

Fat: 9g

# Apple Pie Smoothie

**Prep Time:** 5 minutes

**Cook Time:** 0 minutes

**Total Time:** 5 minutes

**Servings:** 2

**Ingredients:**

- 1 apple, cored and sliced
- 1/2 banana
- 1/2 teaspoon cinnamon
- 1/2 cup almond milk
- 1 tablespoon maple syrup
- 1/2 cup ice

**Preparation Steps:**

1. Pour maple syrup and almond milk into the Vitamix.
2. Combine the banana, cinnamon, apple slices, and apple.
3. Blend on low until completely smooth.
4. Blend in the ice until smooth and creamy.
5. Add a dash of cinnamon before serving.
6. A small amount of maple syrup drizzled on top.

**Nutritional Information (per serving):**

Calories: 180

Protein: 2g

Carbs: 38g

Fat: 3g

# Chocolate Cherry Smoothie

**Prep Time:** 5 minutes

**Cook Time:** 0 minutes

**Total Time:** 5 minutes

**Servings:** 2

**Ingredients:**

- 1 cup frozen cherries
- 1 tablespoon cocoa powder
- 1/2 banana
- 1 cup almond milk
- 1 tablespoon honey
- 1/2 cup ice

**Preparation Steps:**

1. Put the chocolate powder and almond milk into the Vitamix.
2. Incorporate the banana and frozen cherries.
3. To make it sweeter, spoon in some honey.
4. Blend on low until completely smooth.
5. Blend in the ice until smooth and creamy.
6. Sprinkle some chocolate powder on top before serving.

**Nutritional Information (per serving):**

Calories: 190

Protein: 4g

Carbs: 36g

Fat: 5g

# Pear Ginger Smoothie

**Prep Time:** 5 minutes

**Cook Time:** 0 minutes

**Total Time:** 5 minutes

**Servings:** 2

**Ingredients:**

- 1 ripe pear, sliced
- 1/2 teaspoon fresh ginger, grated
- 1/2 banana
- 1/2 cup almond milk
- 1 tablespoon honey
- 1/2 cup ice

**Preparation Steps:**

1. Blend in the Vitamix with the almond milk and ginger.
2. On top of the banana, add the sliced pears.
3. To make it sweeter, spoon in some honey.
4. Blend on low until completely smooth.
5. Blend in the ice until smooth and creamy.
6. Accompany with a delicate pear slice.

**Nutritional Information (per serving):**

Calories: 170

Protein: 2g

Carbs: 34g

Fat: 4g

# Cantaloupe Coconut Smoothie

**Prep Time:** 5 minutes

**Cook Time:** 0 minutes

**Total Time:** 5 minutes

**Servings:** 2

**Ingredients:**

- 1 cup cantaloupe, diced
- 1/2 banana
- 1/2 cup coconut milk
- 1 tablespoon honey
- 1/2 cup ice

**Preparation Steps:**

1. Blend in the Vitamix with the coconut milk included.
2. Incorporate honey, banana, and cantaloupe.
3. Blend on low until completely smooth.
4. Puree the mixture once more after adding ice.
5. Garnish with coconut flakes and serve cold.
6. Finish with a sprig of mint.

**Nutritional Information (per serving):**

Calories: 160

Protein: 2g

Carbs: 28g

Fat: 5g

# Mango Carrot Smoothie

**Prep Time:** 5 minutes

**Cook Time:** 0 minutes

**Total Time:** 5 minutes

**Servings:** 2

**Ingredients:**

- 1/2 cup mango chunks
- 1/2 cup carrot, chopped
- 1/2 banana
- 1/2 cup orange juice
- 1 tablespoon honey
- 1/2 cup ice

**Preparation Steps:**

1. Fill the Vitamix with orange juice.
2. Toss with some honey, mango, carrot, and banana.
3. Blend on low until completely smooth.
4. Blend in the ice until it becomes foamy.
5. Add shredded carrot on top before serving.
6. Immediately savor.

**Nutritional Information (per serving):**

Calories: 170

Protein: 2g

Carbs: 35g

Fat: 1g

# Pineapple Avocado Smoothie

**Prep Time:** 5 minutes

**Cook Time:** 0 minutes

**Total Time:** 5 minutes

**Servings:** 2

**Ingredients:**

- 1/2 cup pineapple chunks
- 1/2 avocado
- 1/2 banana
- 1/2 cup almond milk
- 1 tablespoon lime juice
- 1/2 cup ice

**Preparation Steps:**

1. To the Vitamix, add the almond milk and lime juice.
2. Toss in some bananas, avocados, and pineapple.
3. Blend on low until completely smooth.
4. Puree the mixture once more after adding ice.
5. Garnish each serving with a wedge of lime.
6. For added crunch, top with chia seeds.

**Nutritional Information (per serving):**

Calories: 190

Protein: 3g

Carbs: 26g

Fat: 9g

# Chocolate Mint Smoothie

**Prep Time:** 5 minutes

**Cook Time:** 0 minutes

**Total Time:** 5 minutes

**Servings:** 2

**Ingredients:**

- 1/2 banana
- 1 tablespoon cocoa powder
- 1/2 teaspoon peppermint extract
- 1/2 cup almond milk
- 1 tablespoon honey
- 1/2 cup ice

**Preparation Steps:**

1. Blend in the Vitamix with the almond milk and peppermint essence.
2. Gather the cocoa powder, honey, and bananas.
3. Blend on low until completely smooth.
4. Blend in the ice until it becomes foamy.
5. For garnish, top with a few leaves of fresh mint.
6. Sprinkle chocolate powder on top as a garnish.

**Nutritional Information (per serving):**

Calories: 170

Protein: 3g

Carbs: 28g

Fat: 5g

# Kiwi Banana Smoothie

**Prep Time:** 5 minutes

**Cook Time:** 0 minutes

**Total Time:** 5 minutes

**Servings:** 2

**Ingredients:**

- 2 kiwis, peeled and sliced
- 1 banana
- 1/2 cup Greek yogurt
- 1 tablespoon honey
- 1/2 cup ice

**Preparation Steps:**

1. Blend in some Greek yogurt.
2. Incorporate slices of kiwi, banana, and honey.
3. Blend on low until completely smooth.
4. Blend in the ice until smooth and creamy.
5. Garnish with pieces of kiwi.
6. Have it cold.

**Nutritional Information (per serving):**

Calories: 190

Protein: 5g

Carbs: 30g

Fat: 3g

# Blueberry Oat Smoothie

**Prep Time:** 5 minutes

**Cook Time:** 0 minutes

**Total Time:** 5 minutes

**Servings:** 2

**Ingredients:**

- 1/2 cup frozen blueberries
- 2 tablespoons rolled oats
- 1/2 banana
- 1/2 cup almond milk
- 1 tablespoon maple syrup
- 1/2 cup ice

**Preparation Steps:**

1. Pour maple syrup and almond milk into the Vitamix.
2. Coat the oats with the blueberries and banana.
3. Blend on low until completely smooth.
4. Process until thickened by adding ice.
5. Top with a few oats and serve.
6. What a delicious way to start the day!

**Nutritional Information (per serving):**

Calories: 200

Protcin: 4g

Carbs: 34g

Fat: 4g

# Watermelon Lime Smoothie

**Prep Time:** 5 minutes

**Cook Time:** 0 minutes

**Total Time:** 5 minutes

**Servings:** 2

**Ingredients:**

- 2 cups watermelon, diced
- 1 tablespoon lime juice
- 1 tablespoon honey
- 1/2 cup ice

**Preparation Steps:**

1. You can mix fruit and lime juice in a Vitamix.
2. For sweetness, add honey.
3. Change the speed from low to high and blend until the smooth.
4. Blend in the ice until the drink is icy and slushy.
5. Add lime zest before serving.
6. If it's hot outside, cool off!

**Nutritional Information (per serving):**

Calories: 120

Protein: 2g

Carbs: 28g

Fat: 1g

# Apple Cinnamon Smoothie

**Prep Time:** 5 minutes

**Cook Time:** 0 minutes

**Total Time:** 5 minutes

**Servings:** 2

**Ingredients:**

- 1 apple, cored and sliced
- 1/2 banana
- 1/2 teaspoon cinnamon
- 1/2 cup almond milk
- 1 tablespoon maple syrup
- 1/2 cup ice

**Preparation Steps:**

1. Take out the maple syrup and almond milk.
2. Put in the cinnamon, apple, and banana.
3. Change the speed from low to high and blend until the smooth.
4. Blend with ice until it gets foamy.
5. Serve with cinnamon on top.
6. Add apple pieces as a garnish.

**Nutritional Information (per serving):**

Calories: 170

Protein: 2g

Carbs: 34g

Fat: 3g

# Peach Basil Smoothie

**Prep Time:** 5 minutes

**Cook Time:** 0 minutes

**Total Time:** 5 minutes

**Servings:** 2

**Ingredients:**

- 1 peach, sliced
- 1/2 banana
- 3 basil leaves
- 1/2 cup coconut water
- 1 tablespoon honey
- 1/2 cup ice

**Preparation Steps:**

1. Put the honey and coconut water into the Vitamix.
2. Serve with sliced peaches, bananas, and basil.
3. Blend on low until completely smooth.
4. Blend in the ice until smooth and creamy.
5. Top with a basil leaf and serve.
6. Take pleasure in a revitalizing herbal spin!

**Nutritional Information (per serving):**

Calories: 150

Protein: 2g

Carbs: 30g

Fat: 1g

# Strawberry Watermelon Smoothie

**Prep Time:** 5 minutes

**Cook Time:** 0 minutes

**Total Time:** 5 minutes

**Servings:** 2

**Ingredients:**

- 1 cup watermelon, diced
- 1/2 cup frozen strawberries
- 1/2 banana
- 1 tablespoon lime juice
- 1/2 cup ice

**Preparation Steps:**

1. Fill the Vitamix with lime juice and watermelon.
2. Include the banana and strawberries.
3. Blend on low until completely smooth.
4. Puree with ice until thick and invigorating.
5. Drizzle a strawberry over top before serving.
6. Savor the icy taste!

**Nutritional Information (per serving):**

Calories: 130

Protein: 2g

Carbs: 28g

Fat: 1g

# Blackberry Banana Smoothie

**Prep Time:** 5 minutes

**Cook Time:** 0 minutes

**Total Time:** 5 minutes

**Servings:** 2

**Ingredients:**

- 1/2 cup blackberries
- 1 banana
- 1/2 cup Greek yogurt
- 1 tablespoon honey
- 1/2 cup almond milk
- 1/2 cup ice

**Preparation Steps:**

1. To the Vitamix, add honey and almond milk.
2. Include banana, blackberries, and Greek yogurt.
3. Blend on low until completely smooth.
4. Blend in the ice until smooth and creamy.
5. Add some blackberries on top before serving.
6. Have it cold.

**Nutritional Information (per serving):**

Calories: 200

Protein: 6g

Carbs: 32g

Fat: 4g

# Tropical Sunrise Smoothie

**Prep Time:** 5 minutes

**Cook Time:** 0 minutes

**Total Time:** 5 minutes

**Servings:** 2

**Ingredients:**

- 1/2 cup pineapple chunks
- 1/2 cup mango chunks
- 1/2 orange, peeled
- 1 tablespoon coconut milk
- 1 tablespoon honey
- 1/2 cup ice

**Preparation Steps:**

1. Combine the honey and coconut milk in the Vitamix.
2. Mango, pineapple, and orange should be added.
3. Blend on low until completely smooth.
4. Blend in ice till it becomes tropical and foamy.
5. Accompany with a wedge of pineapple.
6. Take it easy on that island!

**Nutritional Information (per serving):**

Calories: 170

Protein: 2g

Carbs: 36g

Fat: 2g

# Cherry Almond Smoothie

**Prep Time:** 5 minutes

**Cook Time:** 0 minutes

**Total Time:** 5 minutes

**Servings:** 2

**Ingredients:**

- 1/2 cup cherries, pitted
- 1 banana
- 1 tablespoon almond butter
- 1/2 cup almond milk
- 1 tablespoon maple syrup
- 1/2 cup ice

**Preparation Steps:**

1. Pour maple syrup and almond milk into the Vitamix.
2. Incorporate almond butter, bananas, and cherries.
3. Blend on low until completely smooth.
4. Blend in the ice until it becomes thick and creamy.
5. Top with sliced almonds and serve.
6. Snack on it lavishly.

**Nutritional Information (per serving):**

Calories: 220

Protein: 5g

Carbs: 30g

Fat: 8g

# Spinach Apple Smoothie

**Prep Time:** 5 minutes

**Cook Time:** 0 minutes

**Total Time:** 5 minutes

**Servings:** 2

**Ingredients:**

- 1 cup spinach
- 1 apple, cored and sliced
- 1/2 banana
- 1/2 cup water
- 1 tablespoon honey
- 1/2 cup ice

**Preparation Steps:**

1. Pour honey and water into the Vitamix.
2. Incorporate banana, apple, and spinach.
3. Blend on low until completely smooth.
4. Puree with ice till very verdant.
5. Top with a garnish of spinach leaves and serve.
6. Embrace the healthy boost!

**Nutritional Information (per serving):**

Calories: 140

Protein: 2g

Carbs: 32g

Fat: 1g

# Pear Ginger Smoothie

**Prep Time:** 5 minutes

**Cook Time:** 0 minutes

**Total Time:** 5 minutes

**Servings:** 2

**Ingredients:**

- 1 pear, sliced
- 1/2 banana
- 1/2 teaspoon grated ginger
- 1/2 cup almond milk
- 1 tablespoon honey
- 1/2 cup ice

**Preparation Steps:**

1. To the Vitamix, add honey and almond milk.
2. Toss in some ginger, banana, and pear.
3. Blend on low until completely smooth.
4. Blend in the ice until smooth and creamy.
5. Garnish with cinnamon before serving.
6. Simmer in a warm zing!

**Nutritional Information (per serving):**

Calories: 160

Protein: 2g

Carbs: 32g

Fat: 3g

# Strawberry Kiwi Smoothie

**Prep Time:** 5 minutes

**Cook Time:** 0 minutes

**Total Time:** 5 minutes

**Servings:** 2

**Ingredients:**

- 1/2 cup frozen strawberries
- 2 kiwis, peeled and sliced
- 1/2 banana
- 1/2 cup coconut water
- 1 tablespoon honey
- 1/2 cup ice

**Preparation Steps:**

1. Put the honey and coconut water into the Vitamix.
2. Incorporate banana, kiwi, and strawberries.
3. Blend on low until completely smooth.
4. Puree with ice till cold and revitalizing.
5. Garnish with pieces of kiwi.
6. Get lost in the tropics.

**Nutritional Information (per serving):**

Calories: 150

Protein: 2g

Carbs: 28g

Fat: 1g

# Blueberry Pomegranate Smoothie

**Prep Time:** 5 minutes

**Cook Time:** 0 minutes

**Total Time:** 5 minutes

**Servings:** 2

**Ingredients:**

- 1/2 cup blueberries
- 1/2 cup pomegranate juice
- 1/2 banana
- 1/2 cup Greek yogurt
- 1/2 cup ice

**Preparation Steps:**

1. Pour the yogurt and pomegranate juice into the Vitamix.
2. Incorporate bananas and blueberries.
3. Blend on low until completely smooth.
4. Puree with ice until creamy.
5. Add some pomegranate seeds before serving.
6. Embrace the transformative power of antioxidants!

**Nutritional Information (per serving):**

Calories: 180

Protein: 5g

Carbs: 30g

Fat: 2g

# Banana Nut Smoothie

**Prep Time:** 5 minutes

**Cook Time:** 0 minutes

**Total Time:** 5 minutes

**Servings:** 2

**Ingredients:**

- 1 banana
- 1 tablespoon peanut butter
- 1/2 cup almond milk
- 1 tablespoon maple syrup
- 1/2 teaspoon cinnamon
- 1/2 cup ice

**Preparation Steps:**

1. Pour maple syrup and almond milk into the Vitamix.
2. Scatter cinnamon, peanut butter, and banana over top.
3. Blend on low until completely smooth.
4. Process until thickened by adding ice.
5. Top with almonds and chopped peanuts.
6. Savour the full-bodied, nutty taste!

**Nutritional Information (per serving):**

Calories: 220

Protein: 5g

Carbs: 26g

Fat: 10g

# Raspberry Lemon Smoothie

**Prep Time:** 5 minutes

**Cook Time:** 0 minutes

**Total Time:** 5 minutes

**Servings:** 2

**Ingredients:**

- 1/2 cup raspberries
- 1/2 banana
- 1 tablespoon lemon juice
- 1/2 cup coconut water
- 1 tablespoon honey
- 1/2 cup ice

**Preparation Steps:**

1. Blend in the Vitamix with the coconut water and lemon juice.
2. Gently incorporate the banana, raspberries, and honey.
3. Blend on low until completely smooth.
4. Blend in the ice until it becomes foamy.
5. Complement with a twist of lemon.
6. Get ready for a burst of flavor!

**Nutritional Information (per serving):**

Calories: 140

Protein: 2g

Carbs: 28g

Fat: 1g

# Coconut Pineapple Smoothie

**Prep Time:** 5 minutes

**Cook Time:** 0 minutes

**Total Time:** 5 minutes

**Servings:** 2

**Ingredients:**

- 1/2 cup pineapple chunks
- 1/2 banana
- 1/2 cup coconut milk
- 1 tablespoon shredded coconut
- 1 tablespoon honey
- 1/2 cup ice

**Preparation Steps:**

1. Combine the honey and coconut milk in the Vitamix.
2. Shred the coconut and mix with the pineapple and banana.
3. Blend on low until completely smooth.
4. Combine with ice and process until smooth and delicious.
5. Top with additional coconut before serving.
6. Indulge in a tropical vacation!

**Nutritional Information (per serving):**

Calories: 190

Protein: 2g

Carbs: 30g

Fat: 7g

# Cucumber Mint Smoothie

**Prep Time:** 5 minutes

**Cook Time:** 0 minutes

**Total Time:** 5 minutes

**Servings:** 2

**Ingredients:**

- 1/2 cucumber, peeled and sliced
- 1/2 cup Greek yogurt
- 1 tablespoon honey
- 5 mint leaves
- 1/2 cup water
- 1/2 cup ice

**Preparation Steps:**

1. Pour honey and water into the Vitamix.
2. Then, combine the cucumber, Greek yogurt, and mint leaves.
3. Blend on low until completely smooth.
4. Puree with ice till cold and revitalizing.
5. Put some mint over top and serve.
6. Savor the refreshing crunch!

**Nutritional Information (per serving):**

Calories: 120

Protein: 5g

Carbs: 14g

Fat: 3g

# Chocolate Avocado Smoothie

**Prep Time:** 5 minutes

**Cook Time:** 0 minutes

**Total Time:** 5 minutes

**Servings:** 2

**Ingredients:**

- 1/2 avocado
- 1 banana
- 1 tablespoon cocoa powder
- 1 tablespoon honey
- 1/2 cup almond milk
- 1/2 cup ice

**Preparation Steps:**

1. Pour honey and almond milk into the Vitamix.
2. Add the banana, avocado, and cocoa powder.
3. Turn the blender up to high until it's creamy.
4. Blend with ice until smooth.
5. Sprinkle with chocolate powder and serve.
6. Savor the deliciousness of chocolate!

**Nutritional Information (per serving):**

Calories: 240

Protein: 4g

Carbs: 26g

Fat: 12g

**Prep Time:** 5 minutes

**Cook Time:** 0 minutes

**Total Time:** 5 minutes

**Servings:** 2

**Ingredients:**

- 1 cup mango chunks
- 1/2 cup coconut milk
- 1 tablespoon honey
- 1/2 banana
- 1/2 cup ice

**Preparation Steps:**

1. Pour honey and coconut milk into the Vitamix.
2. Add the banana and mango.
3. Smoothly blend on low to high.
4. Blend till creamy after adding ice.
5. Garnish with coconut flakes.
6. Savor the tropical atmosphere!

**Nutritional Information (per serving):**

Calories: 190

Protein: 2g

Carbs: 30g

Fat: 6g

# Pineapple Kale Smoothie
**Prep Time:** 5 minutes

**Cook Time:** 0 minutes

**Total Time:** 5 minutes

**Servings:** 2

**Ingredients:**

- 1 cup kale leaves
- 1/2 cup pineapple chunks
- 1/2 banana
- 1/2 cup coconut water
- 1 tablespoon honey
- 1/2 cup ice

**Preparation Steps:**

1. Pour honey and coconut water into the Vitamix.
2. Add the banana, pineapple, and greens.
3. Smoothly blend on low to high.
4. Blend with ice till bright.
5. Garnish with pineapple and serve.
6. Savor some revitalizing greens!

**Nutritional Information (per serving):**

Calories: 150

Protein: 3g

Carbs: 28g

Fat: 1g

## Peanut Butter Banana Smoothie

**Prep Time:** 5 minutes

**Cook Time:** 0 minutes

**Total Time:** 5 minutes

**Servings:** 2

**Ingredients:**

- 1 banana
- 1 tablespoon peanut butter
- 1/2 cup almond milk
- 1 tablespoon honey
- 1/2 teaspoon cinnamon
- 1/2 cup ice

**Preparation Steps:**

1. Pour honey and almond milk into the Vitamix.
2. Add the cinnamon, peanut butter, and banana.
3. Turn the blender up to high until it's creamy.
4. Blend with ice until thick.
5. Garnish with cinnamon and serve.
6. Savor the ultimate in comfort!

**Nutritional Information (per serving):**

Calories: 230

Protein: 5g

Carbs: 26g

Fat: 10g

# Carrot Mango Smoothie

**Prep Time:** 5 minutes

**Cook Time:** 0 minutes

**Total Time:** 5 minutes

**Servings:** 2

**Ingredients:**

- 1/2 cup carrot juice
- 1 cup mango chunks
- 1/2 banana
- 1 tablespoon honey
- 1/2 cup ice

**Preparation Steps:**

1. Fill the Vitamix with carrot juice and honey.
2. Add the banana and mango.
3. Smoothly blend on low to high.
4. Blend with ice till bright.
5. Garnish with carrot sticks and serve.
6. Savor a vibrant beverage!

**Nutritional Information (per serving):**

Calories: 160

Protein: 2g

Carbs: 32g

Fat: 1g

# Watermelon Strawberry Smoothie

**Prep Time:** 5 minutes

**Cook Time:** 0 minutes

**Total Time:** 5 minutes

**Servings:** 2

**Ingredients:**

- 1 cup watermelon chunks
- 1/2 cup strawberries
- 1/2 banana
- 1 tablespoon lime juice
- 1/2 cup ice

**Preparation Steps:**

1. Fill the Vitamix with lime juice.
2. Add the banana, strawberries, and watermelon.
3. Smoothly blend on low to high.
4. Blend with ice until frosted.
5. Serve with a wedge of lime.
6. Savor the sweetness of summer!

**Nutritional Information (per serving):**

Calories: 110

Protein: 1g

Carbs: 24g

Fat: 0g

## Beet Berry Smoothie

**Prep Time:** 5 minutes

**Cook Time:** 0 minutes

**Total Time:** 5 minutes

**Servings:** 2

**Ingredients:**

- 1 small cooked beet, chopped
- 1/2 cup mixed berries
- 1/2 banana
- 1/2 cup orange juice
- 1/2 cup ice

## Preparation Steps:

1. In Vitamix, add orange juice.
2. Add the banana, berries, and beets.
3. Smoothly blend on low to high.
4. Blend with ice till bright.
5. Garnish with berries and serve.
6. Savor earthy deliciousness!

## Nutritional Information (per serving):

Calories: 150

Protein: 2g

Carbs: 32g

Fat: 0g

# Green Tea Mango Smoothie

**Prep Time:** 5 minutes

**Cook Time:** 0 minutes

**Total Time:** 5 minutes

**Servings:** 2

**Ingredients:**

- 1/2 cup brewed green tea, cooled
- 1 cup mango chunks

- 1/2 banana
- 1 tablespoon honey
- 1/2 cup ice

## Preparation Steps:

1. Fill the Vitamix with green tea and honey.
2. Add the banana and mango.
3. Smoothly blend on low to high.
4. Blend until refreshed after adding ice.
5. Garnish with mint leaves.
6. Savor a revitalizing drink!

## Nutritional Information (per serving):

Calories: 140

Protein: 1g

Carbs: 30g

Fat: 0g

# Pumpkin Spice Smoothie

**Prep Time:** 5 minutes

**Cook Time:** 0 minutes

**Total Time:** 5 minutes

**Servings:** 2

**Ingredients:**

- 1/2 cup pumpkin puree
- 1 banana
- 1/2 teaspoon pumpkin pie spice
- 1/2 cup almond milk

- 1 tablespoon maple syrup
- 1/2 cup ice

## Preparation Steps:

1. Pour maple syrup and almond milk into the Vitamix.
2. Add the pumpkin pie spice, banana, and pumpkin.
3. Smoothly blend on low to high.
4. Blend till creamy after adding ice.
5. Sprinkle with cinnamon and serve.
6. Savor the flavors of fall!

## Nutritional Information (per serving):

Calories: 160

Protein: 2g

Carbs: 30g

Fat: 3g

# Blackberry Vanilla Smoothie

**Prep Time:** 5 minutes

**Cook Time:** 0 minutes

**Total Time:** 5 minutes

**Servings:** 2

**Ingredients:**

- 1/2 cup blackberries
- 1 banana
- 1/2 teaspoon vanilla extract
- 1/2 cup Greek yogurt
- 1/2 cup almond milk

- 1/2 cup ice

## Preparation Steps:

1. Pour vanilla and almond milk into the Vitamix.
2. Add Greek yogurt, banana, and blackberries.
3. Smoothly blend on low to high.
4. Blend till creamy after adding ice.
5. Add some fresh berries on top.
6. Savor a delicious treat!

## Nutritional Information (per serving):

Calories: 160

Protein: 5g

Carbs: 24g

Fat: 4g

## Papaya Pineapple Smoothie

**Prep Time:** 5 minutes

**Cook Time:** 0 minutes

**Total Time:** 5 minutes

**Servings:** 2

## Ingredients:

- 1/2 cup papaya chunks
- 1/2 cup pineapple chunks
- 1/2 banana
- 1/2 cup orange juice
- 1/2 cup ice

**Preparation Steps:**

1. In Vitamix, add orange juice.
2. Add the banana, papaya, and pineapple.
3. Smoothly blend on low to high.
4. Blend until tropical after adding ice.
5. Serve with a wedge of pineapple.
6. Savor flavors from around the world!

**Nutritional Information (per serving):**

Calories: 140

Protein: 1g

Carbs: 30g

Fat: 0g

# Almond Berry Protein Smoothie

**Prep Time:** 5 minutes

**Cook Time:** 0 minutes

**Total Time:** 5 minutes

**Servings:** 2

**Ingredients:**

- 1/2 cup mixed berries
- 1 tablespoon almond butter
- 1 scoop vanilla protein powder
- 1/2 cup almond milk
- 1/2 cup ice

**Preparation Steps:**

1. Fill the Vitamix with almond milk.
2. Add protein powder, almond butter, and berries.
3. Smoothly blend on low to high.
4. Blend with ice until thick.
5. Add almond flakes on top.
6. Savor a blast of protein!

**Nutritional Information (per serving):**

Calories: 220

Protein: 15g

Carbs: 18g

Fat: 8g

# Cinnamon Apple Smoothie

**Prep Time:** 5 minutes

**Cook Time:** 0 minutes

**Total Time:** 5 minutes

**Servings:** 2

**Ingredients:**

- 1 apple, chopped
- 1/2 banana
- 1/2 teaspoon cinnamon
- 1/2 cup Greek yogurt
- 1/2 cup almond milk
- 1/2 cup ice

**Preparation Steps:**

1. Fill the Vitamix with almond milk.

2. Add Greek yogurt, banana, apple, and cinnamon.
3. Smoothly blend on low to high.
4. Blend till creamy after adding ice.
5. Sprinkle with cinnamon and serve.
6. Savor comfortable coziness!

**Nutritional Information (per serving):**

Calories: 180

Protein: 5g

Carbs: 28g

Fat: 3g

## Spinach Peach Smoothie

**Prep Time:** 5 minutes

**Cook Time:** 0 minutes

**Total Time:** 5 minutes

**Servings:** 2

**Ingredients:**

- 1 cup spinach
- 1/2 cup peach slices
- 1/2 banana
- 1/2 cup coconut water
- 1/2 cup ice

**Preparation Steps:**

1. Fill the Vitamix with coconut water.
2. Add the banana, peach, and spinach.
3. Blend until vivid, ranging from low to high.

4. Blend with ice until fresh.
5. Serve with slices of peach.
6. Savor the green vibrancy!

**Nutritional Information (per serving):**

Calories: 130

Protein: 2g

Carbs: 26g

Fat: 1g

## Mocha Smoothie

**Prep Time:** 5 minutes

**Cook Time:** 0 minutes

**Total Time:** 5 minutes

**Servings:** 2

**Ingredients:**

- 1/2 cup cold brewed coffee
- 1/2 banana
- 1 tablespoon cocoa powder
- 1 tablespoon maple syrup
- 1/2 cup almond milk
- 1/2 cup ice

**Preparation Steps:**

1. Fill the Vitamix with coffee, almond milk, and maple syrup.
2. Add the chocolate powder and banana.
3. Turn the blender up to high until it's creamy.
4. Blend with ice until frosted.

5. Dust with chocolate and serve.
6. Savor the bliss of coffee!

**Nutritional Information (per serving):**

Calories: 130

Protein: 2g

Carbs: 22g

Fat: 3g

# Zesty Orange Smoothie

**Prep Time:** 5 minutes

**Cook Time:** 0 minutes

**Total Time:** 5 minutes

**Servings:** 2

**Ingredients:**

- 1 orange, peeled and segmented
- 1/2 banana
- 1/2 cup Greek yogurt
- 1 tablespoon honey
- 1/2 cup ice

**Preparation Steps:**

1. Pour yogurt and honey into the Vitamix.
2. Add banana and orange segments.
3. Blend till bright, going from low to high.
4. Blend with ice until frosted.
5. Garnish with orange zest.
6. Savor the joy of the sun!

**Nutritional Information (per serving):**

Calories: 150

Protein: 5g

Carbs: 28g

Fat: 2g

# Pomegranate Blueberry Smoothie

**Prep Time:** 5 minutes

**Cook Time:** 0 minutes

**Total Time:** 5 minutes

**Servings:** 2

**Ingredients:**

- 1/2 cup pomegranate juice
- 1/2 cup blueberries
- 1/2 banana
- 1/2 cup Greek yogurt
- 1/2 cup ice

**Preparation Steps:**

1. Pour the pomegranate juice into the Vitamix.
2. Greek yogurt, banana, and blueberries should be added.
3. Turn the blender up to high until it's smooth.
4. Blend until vivid after adding ice.
5. With pomegranate seeds, serve.
6. Take advantage of antioxidant power!

**Nutritional Information (per serving):**

Calories: 170

Protein: 5g

Carbs: 28g

Fat: 2g

# Avocado Spinach Smoothie

**Prep Time:** 5 minutes

**Cook Time:** 0 minutes

**Total Time:** 5 minutes

**Servings:** 2

**Ingredients:**

- 1/2 avocado
- 1 cup spinach
- 1/2 banana
- 1/2 cup almond milk
- 1 tablespoon honey
- 1/2 cup ice

**Preparation Steps:**

1. Pour honey and almond milk into the Vitamix.
2. Add the banana, spinach, and avocado.
3. From low to high, blend until smooth.
4. Blend with ice until smooth.
5. Add chia seeds on top.
6. Savor eco-friendly luxury!

**Nutritional Information (per serving):**

Calories: 210

Protein: 3g

Carbs: 20g

Fat: 12g

## Ginger Pear Smoothie

**Prep Time:** 5 minutes

**Cook Time:** 0 minutes

**Total Time:** 5 minutes

**Servings:** 2

**Ingredients:**

- 1 pear, cored and chopped
- 1/2 banana
- 1/2 teaspoon grated ginger
- 1/2 cup Greek yogurt
- 1/2 cup almond milk
- 1/2 cup ice

**Preparation Steps:**

1. Fill the Vitamix with Greek yogurt and almond milk.
2. Add the ginger, banana, and pear.
3. Turn the blender up to high until it's creamy.
4. Blend with ice until smooth.
5. Serve with a piece of ginger.
6. Savor some spicy sweetness!

**Nutritional Information (per serving):**

Calories: 170

Protein: 5g

Carbs: 26g

Fat: 3g

# Cantaloupe Coconut Smoothie

**Prep Time:** 5 minutes

**Cook Time:** 0 minutes

**Total Time:** 5 minutes

**Servings:** 2

**Ingredients:**

- 1 cup cantaloupe, cubed
- 1/2 banana
- 1/2 cup coconut milk
- 1 tablespoon shredded coconut
- 1/2 cup ice

**Preparation Steps:**

1. Put the shredded coconut and coconut milk in the Vitamix.
2. Add the banana and cantaloupe.
3. Smoothly blend on low to high.
4. Blend till creamy after adding ice.
5. Garnish with coconut.
6. Savor the sweetness of the tropics!

**Nutritional Information (per serving):**

Calories: 160

Protein: 2g

Carbs: 20g

Fat: 7g

# Cherry Almond Smoothie

**Prep Time:** 5 minutes

**Cook Time:** 0 minutes

**Total Time:** 5 minutes

**Servings:** 2

**Ingredients:**

- 1/2 cup cherries, pitted
- 1/2 banana
- 1 tablespoon almond butter
- 1/2 cup almond milk
- 1/2 cup ice

**Preparation Steps:**

1. Fill the Vitamix with almond butter and milk.
2. Add the banana and cherries.
3. Blend till delightful, ranging from low to high.
4. Blend with ice until frosted.
5. Serve with pieces of almond.
6. Savor the depth of flavor!

**Nutritional Information (per serving):**

Calories: 190

Protein: 4g

Carbs: 24g

Fat: 8g

# Creamy Strawberry Oat Smoothie

**Prep Time:** 5 minutes

**Cook Time:** 0 minutes

**Total Time:** 5 minutes

**Servings:** 2

**Ingredients:**

- 1/2 cup strawberries
- 1/2 banana
- 2 tablespoons rolled oats
- 1/2 cup Greek yogurt
- 1/2 cup almond milk
- 1/2 cup ice

**Preparation Steps:**

1. Fill the Vitamix with Greek yogurt and almond milk.
2. Add the oats, banana, and strawberries.
3. Turn the blender up to high until it's creamy.
4. Blend with ice until thick.
5. Sprinkle with oats and serve.
6. Savor hearty goodness!

**Nutritional Information (per serving):**

Calories: 210

Protein: 7g

Carbs: 28g

Fat: 5g

# Kiwi Spinach Smoothie

**Prep Time:** 5 minutes

**Cook Time:** 0 minutes

**Total Time:** 5 minutes

**Servings:** 2

**Ingredients:**

- 2 kiwis, peeled
- 1/2 banana
- 1 cup spinach
- 1/2 cup coconut water
- 1/2 cup ice

**Preparation Steps:**

1. Fill the Vitamix with coconut water.
2. Add the banana, spinach, and kiwi.
3. Blend until vivid, ranging from low to high.
4. Blend until refreshed after adding ice.
5. Serve with chunks of kiwi.
6. Savor nutritious food!

**Nutritional Information (per serving):**

Calories: 140

Protein: 2g

Carbs: 28g

Fat: 0g

# Lemon Blueberry Smoothie

**Prep Time:** 5 minutes

**Cook Time:** 0 minutes

**Total Time:** 5 minutes

**Servings:** 2

**Ingredients:**

- 1/2 cup blueberries
- 1/2 banana
- 1/2 lemon, juiced
- 1/2 cup Greek yogurt
- 1/2 cup almond milk
- 1/2 cup ice

**Preparation Steps:**

1. Pour lemon juice and almond milk into the Vitamix.
2. Add the yogurt, banana, and blueberries.
3. Smoothly blend on low to high.
4. Blend with ice until cooled.
5. Serve with the zest of a lemon.
6. Savor the zesty freshness!

**Nutritional Information (per serving):**

Calories: 170

Protein: 5g

Carbs: 26g

Fat: 3g

# Avocado Mango Smoothie

**Prep Time:** 5 minutes

**Cook Time:** 0 minutes

**Total Time:** 5 minutes

**Servings:** 2

**Ingredients:**

- 1/2 avocado
- 1/2 cup mango chunks
- 1/2 banana
- 1/2 cup orange juice
- 1/2 cup ice

**Preparation Steps:**

1. In Vitamix, add orange juice.
2. Add the banana, mango, and avocado.
3. From low to high, blend until smooth.
4. Blend with ice until thick.
5. Serve with cubed mango.
6. Savor the creamy sunlight!

**Nutritional Information (per serving):**

Calories: 210

Protein: 2g

Carbs: 28g

Fat: 10g

# Raspberry Lime Smoothie

**Prep Time:** 5 minutes

**Cook Time:** 0 minutes

**Total Time:** 5 minutes

**Servings:** 2

**Ingredients:**

- 1/2 cup raspberries
- 1/2 banana
- 1/2 lime, juiced
- 1 tablespoon honey
- 1/2 cup almond milk
- 1/2 cup ice

**Preparation Steps:**

1. Pour honey and almond milk into the Vitamix.
2. Add the lime juice, banana, and raspberries.
3. Blend till bright, going from low to high.
4. Blend with ice till bright.
5. Serve with slices of lime.
6. Savor tart delight!

**Nutritional Information (per serving):**

Calories: 150

Protein: 2g

Carbs: 28g

Fat: 2g

## Chocolate Peanut Butter Smoothie

**Prep Time:** 5 minutes

**Cook Time:** 0 minutes

**Total Time:** 5 minutes

**Servings:** 2

**Ingredients:**

- 1/2 banana
- 1 tablespoon peanut butter
- 1 tablespoon cocoa powder
- 1/2 cup almond milk
- 1 scoop chocolate protein powder
- 1/2 cup ice

**Preparation Steps:**

1. Fill the Vitamix with almond milk.
2. Add the protein powder, banana, peanut butter, and chocolate.
3. Smoothly blend on low to high.
4. Blend with ice until thick.
5. Drizzle with chocolate and serve.
6. Savor luxurious delight!

**Nutritional Information (per serving):**

Calories: 260

Protein: 18g

Carbs: 18g

Fat: 12g

# Peach Basil Smoothie

**Prep Time:** 5 minutes

**Cook Time:** 0 minutes

**Total Time:** 5 minutes

**Servings:** 2

**Ingredients:**

- 1/2 cup peaches, sliced
- 1/2 banana
- 2-3 fresh basil leaves
- 1/2 cup Greek yogurt
- 1/2 cup almond milk
- 1/2 cup ice

**Preparation Steps:**

1. Fill the Vitamix with Greek yogurt and almond milk.
2. Add the basil, banana, and peaches.
3. Turn the heat up to high and blend until aromatic.
4. Blend with ice until smooth.
5. Garnish with basil and serve.
6. Savor the thrill of a fresh garden!

**Nutritional Information (per serving):**

Calories: 170

Protein: 6g

Carbs: 24g

Fat: 3g

# Carrot Orange Ginger Smoothie

**Prep Time:** 5 minutes

**Cook Time:** 0 minutes

**Total Time:** 5 minutes

**Servings:** 2

**Ingredients:**

- 1/2 cup carrot, shredded
- 1/2 cup orange juice
- 1/2 banana
- 1/2 teaspoon grated ginger
- 1/2 cup Greek yogurt
- 1/2 cup ice

**Preparation Steps:**

1. Fill the Vitamix with Greek yogurt and orange juice.
2. Add the ginger, banana, and carrots.
3. Blend till bright, going from low to high.
4. Blend with ice until smooth.
5. Garnish with ginger and serve.
6. Savor a tangy surge!

**Nutritional Information (per serving):**

Calories: 160

Protein: 5g

Carbs: 26g

Fat: 2g

# Pineapple Spinach Smoothie

**Prep Time:** 5 minutes

**Cook Time:** 0 minutes

**Total Time:** 5 minutes

**Servings:** 2

**Ingredients:**

- 1/2 cup pineapple chunks
- 1 cup spinach
- 1/2 banana
- 1/2 cup coconut water
- 1/2 cup ice

**Preparation Steps:**

1. Fill the Vitamix with coconut water.
2. Add pineapple, spinach, and banana.
3. Blend until vivid, ranging from low to high.
4. Blend with ice until cooled.
5. Serve with pineapple garnish.
6. Enjoy fresh greens!

**Nutritional Information (per serving):**

Calories: 140

Protein: 2g

Carbs: 28g

Fat: 0g

# Blackberry Mint Smoothie

**Prep Time:** 5 minutes

**Cook Time:** 0 minutes

**Total Time:** 5 minutes

**Servings:** 2

**Ingredients:**

- 1/2 cup blackberries
- 1/2 banana
- 3-4 fresh mint leaves
- 1/2 cup almond milk
- 1/2 cup Greek yogurt
- 1/2 cup ice

**Preparation Steps:**

1. Fill the Vitamix with Greek yogurt and almond milk.
2. Add the mint, banana, and blackberries.
3. Turn the heat up to high and blend until aromatic.
4. Blend till creamy after adding ice.
5. Serve with a sprig of mint.
6. Savor the freshness of the berries!

**Nutritional Information (per serving):**

Calories: 160

Protein: 5g

Carbs: 22g

Fat: 3g

# Orange Cream Smoothie

**Prep Time:** 5 minutes

**Cook Time:** 0 minutes

**Total Time:** 5 minutes

**Servings:** 2

**Ingredients:**

- 1/2 cup orange juice
- 1/2 banana
- 1/2 cup Greek yogurt
- 1 teaspoon vanilla extract
- 1/2 cup ice

**Preparation Steps:**

1. Fill the Vitamix with Greek yogurt and orange juice.
2. Add vanilla and banana.
3. From low to high, blend until smooth.
4. Blend with ice until smooth.
5. Serve with a piece of orange.
6. Savor some creamy citrus!

**Nutritional Information (per serving):**

Calories: 150

Protein: 5g

Carbs: 22g

Fat: 2g

# Mango Lime Smoothie

**Prep Time:** 5 minutes

**Cook Time:** 0 minutes

**Total Time:** 5 minutes

**Servings:** 2

**Ingredients:**

- 1/2 cup mango chunks
- 1/2 banana
- 1/2 lime, juiced
- 1/2 cup coconut milk
- 1/2 cup ice

**Preparation Steps:**

1. Pour lime juice and coconut milk into the Vitamix.
2. Add the banana and mango.
3. Smoothly blend on low to high.
4. Blend with ice until frosted.
5. Garnish with the zest of the lime.
6. Savor the zest of the tropics!

**Nutritional Information (per serving):**

Calories: 180

Protein: 2g

Carbs: 28g

Fat: 7g

# Peanut Butter Banana Smoothie

**Prep Time:** 5 minutes

**Cook Time:** 0 minutes

**Total Time:** 5 minutes

**Servings:** 2

**Ingredients:**

- 1 banana
- 2 tablespoons peanut butter
- 1/2 cup almond milk
- 1 scoop vanilla protein powder
- 1/2 cup ice

**Preparation Steps:**

1. Fill the Vitamix with almond milk.
2. Add the protein powder, peanut butter, and banana.
3. Turn the blender up to high until it's creamy.
4. Blend with ice until thick.
5. Add peanut drizzle on top.
6. Savor the luscious sweetness!

**Nutritional Information (per serving):**

Calories: 270

Protein: 18g

Carbs: 20g

Fat: 14g

# Blueberry Kale Smoothie

**Prep Time:** 5 minutes

**Cook Time:** 0 minutes

**Total Time:** 5 minutes

**Servings:** 2

**Ingredients:**

- 1/2 cup blueberries
- 1/2 cup kale leaves
- 1/2 banana
- 1/2 cup coconut water
- 1/2 cup ice

**Preparation Steps:**

1. Fill the Vitamix with coconut water.
2. Add the banana, kale, and blueberries.
3. Blend until vivid, ranging from low to high.
4. Blend with ice till brilliant.
5. Add some fresh berries on top.
6. Savor the potent greens!

**Nutritional Information (per serving):**

Calories: 140

Protein: 2g

Carbs: 26g

Fat: 0g

# Cherry Vanilla Smoothie

**Prep Time:** 5 minutes

**Cook Time:** 0 minutes

**Total Time:** 5 minutes

**Servings:** 2

**Ingredients:**

- 1/2 cup cherries, pitted
- 1/2 banana
- 1/2 teaspoon vanilla extract
- 1/2 cup almond milk
- 1/2 cup Greek yogurt
- 1/2 cup ice

**Preparation Steps:**

1. Fill the Vitamix with Greek yogurt and almond milk.
2. Add vanilla, banana, and cherries.
3. Turn the blender up to high until it's creamy.
4. Blend with ice until thick.
5. Garnish with cherries and serve.
6. Savor your lovely comfort!

**Nutritional Information (per serving):**

Calories: 170

Protein: 6g

Carbs: 24g

Fat: 3g

# Apple Cinnamon Smoothie

**Prep Time:** 5 minutes

**Cook Time:** 0 minutes

**Total Time:** 5 minutes

**Servings:** 2

**Ingredients:**

- 1 apple, cored and chopped
- 1/2 banana
- 1/2 teaspoon cinnamon
- 1/2 cup almond milk
- 1/2 cup Greek yogurt
- 1/2 cup ice

**Preparation Steps:**

1. Fill the Vitamix with Greek yogurt and almond milk.
2. Add cinnamon, banana, and apple.
3. Until comfy, blend on low to high.
4. Blend with ice until thick.
5. Sprinkle with cinnamon and serve.
6. Savor coziness with a hint of heat!

**Nutritional Information (per serving):**

Calories: 180

Protein: 6g

Carbs: 26g

Fat: 3g

# Watermelon Mint Smoothie

**Prep Time:** 5 minutes

**Cook Time:** 0 minutes

**Total Time:** 5 minutes

**Servings:** 2

**Ingredients:**

- 1 cup watermelon, cubed
- 1/2 banana
- 3-4 mint leaves
- 1/2 cup coconut water
- 1/2 cup ice

**Preparation Steps:**

1. Fill the Vitamix with coconut water.
2. Add the mint, banana, and watermelon.
3. Turn the blender on and off till it's refreshing.
4. Blend with ice until cooled.
5. Serve with a sprig of mint.
6. Savor some refreshing summertime drinks!

**Nutritional Information (per serving):**

Calories: 120

Protein: 1g

Carbs: 24g

Fat: 0g

# Cucumber Pear Smoothie

**Prep Time:** 5 minutes

**Cook Time:** 0 minutes

**Total Time:** 5 minutes

**Servings:** 2

**Ingredients:**

- 1/2 cup cucumber, chopped
- 1 pear, chopped
- 1/2 banana
- 1/2 cup coconut water
- 1/2 cup ice

**Preparation Steps:**

1. Fill the Vitamix with coconut water.
2. Add the banana, pear, and cucumber.
3. From low to high, blend until smooth.
4. Blend with ice until smooth.
5. Serve with a piece of cucumber.
6. Savor the refreshing freshness!

**Nutritional Information (per serving):**

Calories: 140

Protein: 2g

Carbs: 26g

Fat: 0g

Made in the USA
Coppell, TX
30 May 2025